CONFIRMATION

Anointed and Sealed
with the Spirit

Journal for Adults

Thomas H. Morris and Kathy Coffey

Living the Good News
a division of The Morehouse Group
Denver, CO

Editor: Steve Mueller
Cover Design: Val Price

Scripture quotations taken from the New Revised Standard Version Bible, copyright ©1989 by
the Division of Christian Education of the National Council of Churches of Christ in the USA,
and are used by permission.

Living the Good News
       a division of The Morehouse Group
Editorial Offices
600 Grant Street, Suite 400
Denver, CO 80203
Printed in the United States of America.

ISBN 1-889108-47-2

Table of Contents

Introduction

Your personal reflection recorded in this journal can enrich and enlarge the activities of more formal group sessions. It's another way to absorb and take ownership of confirmation preparation. Use the journal as a channel to explore your own feelings, your past and the reasons that prompt you to seek confirmation now.

How to Use This Resource

— as a candidate

This journal provides you with a personal place for reflection. You may choose to share its contents with another person, such as a sponsor, spouse or friend. Or you may decide to reserve its pages for yourself. Either way, it is a sacred space in which to reveal your own thoughts and feelings as you prepare for confirmation. Use it freely: if a question awakens and stirs you, respond. If a question prompts little response, skip it and move on. Keep it as a record of your preparation, because when you celebrate the sacrament, you will want to look back over the whole process.

Some questions to consider at this time are:
- What leads me to seek confirmation now?
- What are my hopes and expectations as the preparation process begins?
- To whom can I look for strength and support in this preparation?

— as a parent, sponsor or catechist

An old adage of religious education is, "thou shalt not do unto others what thou hast not first done thyself." As you parent, guide or sponsor a young person through the process of sacramental preparation, you may want to explore your own thoughts and feelings about the topics to which you are introducing the candidate. As on any other issue, it is easier to express yourself if you have first clarified where you stand. This is particularly valid for updating yourself in areas of faith development that you may not have considered lately. Then you can speak authentically with a voice of experience to young people who are quick to detect any form of hypocrisy, even the most subtle.

Feel free either to share your journaling with the confirmation candidate, or to keep these pages private. However you choose to use them, may the experience of journaling make this preparation process richer and more fulfilling both for you and your candidate.

A Review of Confirmation

What is the meaning of the sacrament?

The meaning of this sacrament has remained clear over centuries: confirmation gives the Holy Spirit. While the Spirit is given in a unique way, it is not given for the first time; that occurred in baptism. Candidates for confirmation have lived in the faith and promises of the church for many years. But a different context does not invalidate the first baptismal promises. In the same way, a couple who repeats their marriage vows after twenty-five years knows that the context has changed dramatically. But the new context doesn't invalidate the original vows—if anything, the weight of time and experience makes them more meaningful. Similarly, a couple who fall in love initially find that the qualities they've always had are called forth in a new way for parenthood. Thus, the Spirit who is always present continues to make us more like Christ, strengthening us to continue his work.

How have ideas about confirmation changed over time?

Only from the eleventh century onwards was confirmation separated from baptism. Celebrating the two together showed the link between Jesus' own baptism and the outpouring of the Holy Spirit on his mission. Today, when adults and children of catechetical age are initiated into the Catholic church, baptism and confirmation are still celebrated together.

6

In the early church, the bishop imposed hands on and anointed the newly baptized as part of the baptism rite. As Christianity spread, it became difficult for the bishop to anoint numerous converts. This part of the rite was deferred to a later time when the bishop could visit the parish. Gradually, the anointing took on the name *confirmation*, and the candidates, rather than being the newly baptized, were people who had been baptized years before.

To summarize a long subsequent history, the "soldier-of-Christ model" prevailed when many who are now parents were confirmed themselves. Emphasis was placed on maturity; through the sacrament, children became "soldiers of Christ" who would defend the faith.

Today, less emphasis is placed on maturity, since the gift of the Spirit is an abundance that not even the most mature person could ever deserve. We see that God's action, not ours, takes primacy. We celebrate the Spirit active in the lives of all people. Rather than a "graduation," confirmation is simply a part of ongoing conversion within a community of faith. The newly confirmed are part of a larger group who all grow together in grace, a lifelong process.

What is a parent's or sponsor's role?

Consider that you have gained an apprentice. In the traditional sense of that word, the apprentice learned a trade from a master. What you are conveying instead is the way you live as a Christian. That doesn't mean perfection or phony piety. It simply means welcoming a young person into your struggles and joys, your daily drudgery and moments of grace. What gets you through the day? How does looking at your life through the lens of faith make a difference? Why is your involvement with church so important that you'd sacrifice time to make this commitment?

The answers to those three questions may not come in words. But young people are attuned to nonverbals: the ways we tease them, enjoy them, nurture them and challenge them all speak loudly.

They'll pick up the message more from who you are than from anything you do or say.

If you are a sponsor, your commitment tells a young person: "We value you. We want you to be a part of us. Your youthful energy brings vitality to our community. You are a clear sign of God in our midst." If you are an adult candidate, you are also a sign of life to a community that needs fresh insights and new perspectives.

What This Journal Contains

The journal's five units correspond to the five themes of the formal sessions:

1—Baptism and Eucharist
2—The Gift of the Spirit
3—Conformity to Christ
4—Bearing Witness to Christ
5—Reflection on the Experience of the Sacrament (Mystagogy)

Each unit of the adult journal includes these components:

• adult reflection on the theme of the unit, with questions for reflection and space to write in
• connection to the session's activities
• scripture reflection
• questions on the symbol considered in that unit

Baptism and Eucharist

Why begin with baptism? Don't worry that you've stumbled into the wrong room—wanting confirmation preparation, and instead being surprised by another sacrament. If you are preparing yourself or another person for confirmation, a good way to begin is by recognizing the intimate links between all three sacraments of initiation. Through baptism, we become children of God and members of Christ's body on earth, the Church. All our sins are forgiven, and we share in Christ's ministry. Baptism is the source of unity among all Christians. In the early church, candidates for initiation were washed in the water of baptism and sealed with the oil of confirmation in one sacrament. In the eastern church, baptism and confirmation remain one sacrament. In the western church, the two have been separate only since the eleventh century.

In this unit, we'll consider the session activities, scriptures and symbols for baptism and eucharist.

Reflection

Recall a time when you were affirmed: perhaps an unexpected compliment, a phone call, note or visit left you feeling good about yourself. At that moment, your struggles and hassles probably seemed worthwhile. After such an experience, people feel ready to tackle the world.

Now, reflect on water, in whichever form is most meaningful for you. Maybe it's a cold drink after a long hot run. Maybe it's a hot tub, soothing aching muscles at the end of an arduous day, or a swimming pool or fishing hole, a lake, river, ocean or stream... What does rain bring after a long drought? In addition to the obvious benefits like greening the lawn, how does it refresh our spirits? Why do we feel revived by a morning shower or a hot bath?

If we bring the two concepts together, it's helpful to think first from a negative standpoint. What is life like in a dry period when we don't receive affirmations in any form? Why does the term *drought* apply to the spirit as well as to the land? Why is it appropriate that the most barren desert in this country is named Death Valley? What does it mean to enter a watered garden after crossing a wasted landscape? Now take the analogy one step further: What would life be like without Christ? What does the gift of Christ's presence bring to each hour of each day?

According to Mark's gospel, Jesus himself endured the desert after hearing God affirm him as the beloved son: "At once the Spirit drove him out into the desert" (1:12). What did he see and hear in those moments with John at the Jordan that enabled him to endure Satan's temptations in the wasteland?

Interestingly, he was not given a specific mandate, nor any guarantee he would avoid suffering. In that brief time with the Jordan River rushing over his head, its waters swirling around his nostrils and eyes, his mission must have become clearer. The divine words confirmed that whatever he did, he would be loved.

The same assurance comes to us: "this is my beloved daughter or son. In you I am well pleased." The lack of specific direction may bother us. After all, God doesn't say, "Finish your degree," "Pursue a career in computers," or "Spend more time with your family." The words addressed to Jesus and in turn to us are far better: whatever we do, God assures us of abiding and unconditional love.

That impetus calls us to our own unique missions, the tasks marked with our names, that no one else can do. With the assurance of God's presence, we can confront the questions inherent in our baptismal commitments:

To whom are we called?

WE ARE CALLED By our parents

Who calls us?

Jeasus

For what purpose?

THE purpose of cleansing our souls of sin

What similarities do we find in the stories of Jesus' call and ours?
What differences?

That we are also loved, that there is also
unconditional love

What links do we find between our own experience and the story of
Jesus' baptism ?

Activities

How did you feel about the first gathering of your group?

Small group only 4 or 5
very comfortable

In light of that first meeting, what hopes do you have now for confirmation preparation?

THAt I will be more religious, more with one in god - A Better unity between myself + the CHURCH +(Holy spirit)

If you held a discussion of unity amidst diversity in the Catholic community, what thoughts or questions did you bring away from it?

Respond to one or more of the following quotes in the space below:

- "The place God calls you to is the place where your deep gladness and the world's deep hunger meet."

  — *Frederick Buechner, in* A Baptism Sourcebook, *compiled by J. Robert Baker, Larry J. Nyberg and Victoria M. Tufano (Chicago: Liturgy Training Publications, 1993), 8.*

- "In baptism, we are caught up into the divinity of God, into the life of the Risen Christ."

  — *Godfrey Diekmann,* National Catholic Reporter, *29 May 1998, 2.*

- "[Baptism] includes a special anointing of the baby's heart...The heart is anointed as a main organ of the baby's health but also as the place where all its feelings will nest. The prayer intends that the new child will never become trapped, caught, or entangled in false inner networks of negativity, resentment, or destruction toward itself. The blessings also intend that the child will have a fluency of feeling in its life, that its feelings may flow freely and carry its soul out to the world and gather from the world delight and peace."

  — *John O'Donohue,* Anam Cara: A Book of Celtic Wisdom *(New York: HarperCollins, 1997), 6.*

The place we are called to is a deep gladness
I was called to Be Confirmed because of a
higher power in my life to become more
holy

Baptism

Scripture

The symbols of baptism have a rich biblical context and a long history. Read or review the following stories to discover some of the symbolic meanings of water:

- Genesis 6:5–9:17 (Noah builds an ark.)
- Exodus 1–2; 13–15 (The Hebrew people escape slavery through the Red Sea.)
- Exodus 17:1–7 (Moses strikes the rock; water comes forth.)
- 2 Kings 5 (Naaman the leper is cured in the river Jordan.)
- Mark 6:45-52 (Jesus walks on water.)
- Mark 4:35-41 (Jesus calms a storm at sea.)
- John 4 (Jesus and the Samaritan woman talk about living water.)

Looking back in retrospect or forward in anticipation, what does it mean to you to be immersed in the living waters of baptism?

A Beautiful Sacrament of unity with the
the Church — A Wonderful Sacrament to
begin life as a Catholic-Christian to
Install a direction towards religion

Symbols

If you were baptized as an infant, you probably didn't do much reflection at that time on the symbols of baptism. If you are preparing yourself or another person for baptism, or reflecting back on your own baptism, you now have the opportunity to explore their meaning. Remember that symbols communicate across denominational lines. If you were baptized in another tradition, know that many Christian denominations use the same symbols for baptism.

Immersion in Water

Just as we were once born in the rush of amniotic fluid from the mother's womb, so in baptism we are reborn in the waters of life, remade in the image of God. This endless flow of water cleanses our stains and satisfies our thirsts. This gift is one answer to the Samaritan woman's plea:

> "Give me this water, so that I may never be thirsty..." (John 4:15).

In *Words Around the Font*, Gail Ramshaw writes, "Like the sea, matrix to zillions of pieces of life, the liturgy washes us together to Christ. Like the sea, Christ bears us to God. Like the sea, God sustains us with living water. Here is enough life for us all" (Chicago: Liturgy Training Publications, 1994, 58).

At one level, we want to believe in this endless source of God's life, which nothing can drain or exhaust. At another level, we know that human beings are rarely satisfied. No matter how much we drink, we'll grow thirsty again.

How do you reconcile the apparent tension between these two polarities?

We Are given water – unity – washing us together, however we will always have faults and the need for more water

A need to sin and be forgiven and a need to become a better Christian – more Holy

The baptismal liturgy echoes the statement that human beings are made in God's image. While it may take a lifetime to fully realize what this means, reflect on what it means at this point in your life. How does it affect the way you live?

We Are made to be like Christ – to live in his shadow – to be able to be one as close as possible to him – to live his scriptures + teachings. It gives me strength to live my life – in doing the right things

Passing the Light

When we confront the problem of evil, one metaphor we often use is darkness. Crime rates rise at night; we know of dark places within our hearts. Into this darkness we invite Christ to come, and at the Easter Vigil, we proclaim "Christ our Light!" Just as he restored the sight of the blind during his earthly life, so too he helps us begin to see—sometimes in small increments, sometimes in sudden vision.

What do you feel is a darkness within you now?

Not Being Confirmed - knowing that my Spiritual life could Be much Stronger

How do you respond to the image of Christ as light?

That if we follow him we will can Not be Steered into the wrong direction - that he enriches our life - a profound light

Wearing the New Garment

Are you sensitive to clothing or do you know someone who is? If so, you know how relaxed you feel in jeans and a sweatshirt, how formal and responsible you feel wearing a suit. Clothing has symbolic value in the Christian tradition, because we clothe ourselves in Christ. Whatever we see as physical flaws, they are wrapped in grace. The white color represents a freedom from dirty, demeaning work, a liberation to be robed in white as were the people of heaven, described in Revelation 4:4.

Imagine yourself clothed in a glorious white robe, stainless symbol that you have "put on Christ." How does the clothing affect your behavior?

THE clothing would make me act very loving and pure, trying to live in Christs footsteps AND WHAT HE teaches

Bring AN overwhelming joy

These three symbols of baptism recur in the funeral liturgy. The introductory rites begin at the door of the church, where the presider sprinkles the coffin with holy water and says,

> "In the waters of baptism (*Name*) died with Christ and rose with him to new life. May he/she now share with him eternal glory."

Then family members, friends or the minister place the pall, an "echo" of the baptismal garment, on the coffin. Finally, the Easter candle is placed beside the coffin.

Why do you think it's appropriate to have the same symbols speak at the beginning and at the end of our time on earth?

Its important for us at the beginning of life and end of life on-EARTH To Be granted Gods Eternal Glory—that WE ARE Born into unity of CHRIST At Baptism AND ONCE again when WE Die

The Community

Catholic belief in the incarnation means that God's grace is always mediated through human beings. The Christian assembly may seem sleepy, bored, wildly diverse and at times a bit crazy, but its symbolic value as a "cloud of witnesses" transcends these flaws. Warty as it may sometimes seem, it represents Christ's presence on earth for us in this place, at this time.

Reflect on the people who have been important to you, guiding your journey or blessing it to this point in your life. Focus specifically on one or two of them, asking: How did (*Name*) act like Christ for me?

Eucharist

The eucharist provides ongoing nurture for our life as Christians. It intensifies our union with Christ and other people, and serves as the continued source of unity for all Christians.

Scripture

Become familiar with key scripture texts about the eucharist to discover what the Judeo-Christian tradition believes about the meaning of bread and wine:

- Genesis 14:17-20 (After Abram's military victory, the priest Melchizedek blesses him and offers God bread and wine.)
- Isaiah 55:1-3 (God promises to nourish the people.)
- Exodus 16:1-15 (God feeds the people with manna in the desert.)
- John 6: 1-15, 22-66 (Jesus multiplies loaves and fishes; later he calls himself the bread of life.)
- Matthew 26:26-29; Mark 14:22-25; Luke 22:15-20 (Jesus celebrates his last supper.)
- 1 Corinthians 11:23-26 (Paul describes the Christian eucharistic meal.)

Looking back over these texts, how do they help you understand the meaning of Eucharist?

Symbol

The symbols of hunger and thirst, like those of bread and wine, speak on many levels. In order to appreciate the eucharist, recall a time when:

- You hungered at a physical level.
- You hungered for understanding or affection.

HUNGERED For understanding or Affection now
that I have had Colin

Then recall a time when that hunger was met:

- You were fed physically.
- You received the understanding or affection you needed.

Having Colin — Starting a family

Bread has long been regarded as a staple, a form of sustenance eaten in different forms by people all over the world. Wine, however, is not a necessity, but given for our joy and delight, for celebration more than nurture. Through it Jesus slakes our thirst for creativity and spirit.

For what do you most thirst at this time in your life?

To truely BECOME A BETTER PERSON – A PERSON living CLOSER to the Scriptures. A BETTER CHRISTIAN – ONE who completely understand the faith – says daily Rosary + prayers Along with Reading the Bible – AND most of All living By the scriptures

Recall a time in your life when you really nurtured another person, when you were, in fact, bread and cup for that person. What prompted it?

The word *eucharist* means "to give thanks." Sometimes it's hard to find anything for which to give thanks. But gratitude is a deliberately cultivated habit of Christians, who trust in God's providence and believe in God's graciousness. It corrects our tendency to whine, to ignore what we have and always want more, and to consider ourselves self-sufficient.

Name the five things for which you are most grateful:

ALAN
Colin
TRUE LOVE
FAMILY
OUR HEALTH

(This is a fine practice to continue daily throughout your confirmation preparation, and perhaps throughout your life!)

Prayer

Each chapter ends with a brief example of different prayer forms from the Catholic tradition. If you find a form appealing, try it on your own, with variations. By the time you celebrate confirmation, you will build your own repertoire of prayer forms. Record your memories and impressions after your prayer experience.

Find a quiet place, light a candle if you find it helpful, and choose the prayer you prefer:

> May God support us all the day long,
> till the shadows lengthen
> and the evening comes
> and the busy world is hushed
> and the fever of life is over
> and our work is done—
> then in mercy
> may God give us a safe lodging
> and a holy rest
> and peace at the last.
> —*John Henry Newman*

> Let nothing disturb thee,
> Let nothing affright thee.
> Everything is changing.
> God alone never changes....
> —*St. Teresa of Avila*

The Gift of the Spirit

Reflection

"I will give you a new heart and place a new spirit within you, taking from your bodies your stony hearts and giving you natural hearts."

—Ezekiel 36:26

Transformation may seem like a large concept to wrap the mind around; after all, we don't normally stand on mountaintops and gleam like the sun. But in many subtler ways, we are transformed. As an adult looks back over a lifetime, it's easy to see the passages from infancy to toddlerhood, on to adolescence and maturity. While that perspective may be somewhat truncated for a younger person, it's still possible to observe an extraordinary difference between the helpless infant wailing in the crib and the candidate who confidently drives herself to confirmation gatherings.

If a transformative process is evident on the physical level, how much more powerfully it occurs within us. We grow inwardly from the baby intent on satisfying his own needs into people who care for others. Some powerful grace must be at play as we gradually become capable of setting aside our own needs and wants to honor the needs and wants of others.

As further evidence of this grace, we need only think of how our opinions on controversial issues can change over time. Positions we once held firmly and opinions we once clung to modify and evolve. We are not the same people we were five or ten years ago. Elizabeth Johnson writes in *She Who Is*: the Spirit "has the power to shake up assured certainties and introduce the grace of a new question" (New York: Crossroad, 1993, 138).

> "Then they laid hands on them and they received the holy Spirit" (Acts 8:17).

Part of the genius of Catholic sacraments is the way seemingly unimportant elements can carry vast meaning and weight. Through water flows the saving grace of baptism; through wine and bread, Jesus becomes our nurture. One of the ritual gestures in the celebration of confirmation is the laying on of hands; through the power of human touch, a person is filled with the presence of the Spirit.

The symbolic waters of baptism become more meaningful as we reflect on the ways that water refreshes us daily. We appreciate eucharist more deeply in the context of our own family meals. Similarly, the laying on of hands connects with all the other ways we have been touched. At times when words fail, a touch communicates eloquently. To the recently widowed friend, we don't offer an elaborate rationale—we embrace and weep together. To the child who has fallen and gashed a forehead, we don't lecture—we cleanse the wound gently, apply soothing ointment and give a kiss to make it better. After a stressful day, we usually long for a backrub, not another long-winded speech.

How often a friend's hug has conveyed, "You can tackle this new project!" or "It's wonderful to see you again!" or "I really missed you and I'm glad you're back." Enfolded in another person's arms, we can feel the love of God; we can glimpse the compassion of Jesus. As we send a child off to school or a journey, our final hug conveys, "All strength and blessing go with you." Given what we know of touch and reflecting on its power in our lives, it seems a most fitting gesture for confirmation. How much can be expressed through the touch of human hands.

Questions for Reflection:

What one experience in my life could I point to as evidence of the Spirit's transforming activity?

Baptism
1st Holy Communion
Mass Every Sunday
Colins Baptism
Alan's Election + Soon to Be Baptism, Confirmation + Eucharist

What quality of the Spirit impresses me most, or do I most want to convey to a candidate for confirmation?

Power of the Holy Spirit

Activities

Transformations

The Holy Spirit initiates *transformation* in the believer through baptism. In various ways, including the sacrament of confirmation —the Spirit sustains this *transformation* through the continued outpouring of God's grace.

Encounters with God are always transformative. Since Christians believe we meet God daily, hourly, in every place and time, transformations must then be frequent.

Recall a significant change or transformation in your experience. Describe it here:

Another way of looking at this transformation might be as a movement from one state or situation to a new state or situation, for example:
• from feeling lost to belonging
• from feeling peaceful to being unsettled or discontented

Describe your experience of transformation as one moving from: lost   to: Belonging

Becoming closer to God – & to Alan with his Baptism, Confirmation + Eucharist

What do you learn as you look back on this process?

What an important step in the right direction that we are taking

How does reflecting on this one particular experience help you understand how God transforms you?

How might your understanding of this one experience affect your attitudes toward change in the future?

To HAVE a very positive Attitude to change for the goodness of Christ

Why do you think human beings often resist change or transformation? To what extent is this true of yourself?

Because we just do not like change - especially if it means sacrificing something

this is quite true of myself

St. Paul writes, "We know that all things work together for good for those who love God..." (Rom. 8:28). Hence we can look for the good even in tragedy. When has an experience you dreaded brought unexpected blessing instead?

The Spirit

Some activities in this session concentrated on coming to know the Spirit better through the Spirit's actions. What do you know now about the Spirit?

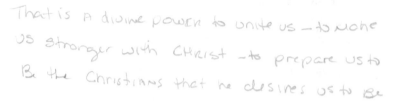

That is A divine power to unite us — to Make us stronger with CHRist — to prepare us to Be the Christians that he desires us to Be

What questions do you still have?

Scripture

When we pray, "Come Holy Spirit," who is this Spirit we invoke? Read the following scripture passages to see how they describe the actions of the Spirit:

- Romans 5:1-2, 5-8
- Romans 8:14-17
- Romans 8:26-27

What was your first impression of these passages?

Using resources provided by the catechist or consulting other scripture commentaries, how does your understanding of these passages change?

What do these passages show about the Spirit?

Symbol

The Laying on of Hands

Recall one experience when touch was for you a sign of healing, love, joy or compassion:

ALANS Comforting touch+ love when my grandmother died

Read one or more of the following scripture passages. Each reveals the power of touch:

- Mark 5:21-24, 35-43 (Jesus heals the daughter of Jairus.)
- Mark 5:25-34 (A sick woman touches Jesus' cloak for healing.)
- Luke 5:12-14 (Jesus touches a leper to heal him.)
- Luke 18:15-17 (Jesus touches children.)
- John 9:1-12 (Jesus cures the man born blind.)
- John 13:3-11 (Jesus washes the feet of the disciples.)
- Acts 8:14-17 (Peter and John give the Holy Spirit by the laying on of hands.)

What was your first impression of your chosen passage(s)?

Using resources from your catechist or consulting other scripture commentaries, how does your understanding of the passage(s) change?

What do you learn about touch from the passage(s)?

The church carries out the mission of Jesus to bring a healing, comforting touch to those who need it. Where do you see God's people doing this, especially in everyday situations of work and home?

OUTREACH programs that are designed to help or aide those less fortunate and in need

In light of what you know about human touch, why do you think the coming of the Spirit in confirmation is symbolized by the laying on of hands?

A comforting touch to symbolize that good is within us that we are soothed or given peace through him

Prayer

For many people, music is an avenue to prayer and making music a prayer in itself. Listen to, sing or reflect on the words of some songs about the Holy Spirit, for example:

- "Send Us Your Spirit" (in *Glory and Praise)*
- "Come Holy Ghost (in *Worship)*
- "Send Us Your Spirit," (in *Gather)*
- "Spirit Blowing through Creation" (in *Gather)*.

Ask your catechist or liturgist for help obtaining the music, or check the song books in your parish.

Conformity to Christ

Reflection

> "Those who love me will keep my word, and my Father will love
> them, and we will come to them and make our home with them."
>
> —*John 14:23*

Homelessness is not solely the plight of the poor. We may see its
physical manifestations on the streets of our cities, in ragged people
pushing shopping carts and lumpy figures sleeping on grates. But a
psychological homelessness seems more pervasive.

We also wander the malls with vacant stares, and haunt the bars, the
entertainment centers, the gaming casinos, searching for meaning or
pleasure. We recognize rootlessness in ourselves as we cast about
for distractions and activities, vaguely unsatisfied but not sure why.
"Give me a place to be, to belong," the chorus cries. "Take me
home."

How deeply Jesus must have understood human longing when he
offered to dwell with us. What does his invitation mean? Our intuitive
sense tells us home is where we drop the load of backpack or brief-
case, dress comfortably, draw on the deep nurture of food and
sleep, become most ourselves, laugh more and relax more completely than anywhere else. It is a place of sustenance for the soul.

It should not, however, be sentimentalized. Home is not the perfect place where all are loved and appreciated. In an era of rampant domestic violence and pervasive child neglect, it's hard to swallow that stereotype.

Home is far from perfect. We may laugh more here, but we also argue more. At this address, we receive the grade reports, the bank overdraft notices and the bills. That's not necessarily bad news, simply a reminder that maintaining a home can be a costly proposition, in psychic resources as well as financial ones.

Perhaps it's there, at the points of intersection for so many lives, that we most often find God. When Jesus dwells with us he will see all our conflicts, all our messiness, all the strains, illness, despair and fatigue. He touches us where it matters most—not ultimately at the office or the church, but at the central core. Begun in love, sprawling with life, our homes are a construct of our deepest selves. We can come to Christ then, not only in formal ritual, but in our oldest clothes, our most casual conversations, our least self-conscious gestures like unloading the dishwasher, mowing the lawn or folding the laundry. There is no need to look for God elsewhere.

The good news that we are joined to Christ by the Spirit and share in Christ's life can center and ground us, give our whole lives direction. When we are marked with the seal of the Spirit, it means God "chose us in Christ, before the foundation of the world, to be holy and without blemish before him" (Ephesians 1:4).

It's hard to understand how we who have failed so often can be the dwelling place of God. Even if we try to believe, our response often sputters into inertia. Somehow the belief never quite makes the transition to action. We know about Christ, but do we know Christ?

The good news is that no matter how miserably we may have squandered that gift, God's grace persists. When candidates are anointed with chrism, they take on Christ's roles as priest, prophet and king. Perhaps not all at once, perhaps not visibly, but the lens of faith reveals that like tattooed soldiers in the Roman army, we bear an indelible mark: we have been claimed. For this life and eternity, we belong to Christ.

Questions for Reflection:

How would I describe my present relationship to Christ?

What feelings and ideas about Christ are most important for my life?

Have I ever felt "psychologically homeless"?

Have I ever experienced what it means to be "at home" in Christ?

If I have in fact been "claimed" for Christ, what difference does it make in the way I lead my life, day to day?

Activities

Who Is Jesus?

Who is Jesus to you? Describe him. What qualities do you find most appealing?

Name people you know or have known in your daily life who share similar characteristics with Jesus.

Sometimes we limit our understanding of Christ's mission to explicitly religious things. Use your newspaper to find signs of need in today's world—and Christlike responses to those needs. List what you find in the space below.

Need   Response

Scripture

Choose one or the other of these passages to work with:

Matthew 5:1-12 — The Beatitudes

In the session, you may have heard and discussed the Beatitudes. Read them again in the quiet and privacy of your home. Then reflect on these questions:

Of all the beatitudes, which one touches you most deeply?

If this text were preached at your funeral, which one would you like emphasized as a beatitude you had practiced?

Where do you see people practicing the Beatitudes, and what do you most admire about their actions?

John 14:23-26 — At Home

Read this passage from Jesus' last supper and reflect on the following:

Recall one person with whom you feel most "at home."

Have you ever tried to create a home for another, others or yourself? Describe that process.

Knowing what you do of being at home, how do you respond to Jesus' promise, "Those who love me will keep my word, and my Father will love them, and we will come to them and make our home with them" (John. 14:23)?

Symbol

The Anointing with Chrism

Think of several ways you use oil in an ordinary day. How is oil essential in that context?

Read one or more of the following scripture passages on anointing.
- 1 Samuel 16:1-13 (Samuel anoints David.)
- Isaiah 61:1-9 (God anoints the servant.)
- John 12:1-8 (Mary anoints Jesus.)
- Ephesians 1:3-4, 13-19 (The Spirit seals the believers.)

What was your initial response to your chosen passage(s)?

Using resources from your catechist or other scripture commentary, how does your understanding of the passage(s) change?

What do you learn about the way oil is used in the Hebrew-Christian tradition from the passage(s)?

The church, when carrying out the mission of Jesus, acts like an anointing with oil: reducing friction, healing, protecting, bringing balm and beauty to human life. Where do you see God's people performing actions that act like oil in the world, in everyday situations of work and home?

In light of what you know about oil, why do you think the rite of confirmation uses an anointing to symbolize God's Spirit?

Prayer

This prayer form is a silent meditation on a scripture passage.

> "I do not call you servants any longer...; I have called you friends..." (John 15:15).

Find a quiet place where you can be uninterrupted for several moments of silence. Meditate on what friendship with Jesus implies.

Bearing Witness to Christ

Reflection

"Some seed fell on good soil, and when it grew, it produced fruit a hundredfold."

—Luke 8:8a

"God has a dream for you," said St. Ignatius of Loyola. For adults, who look in retrospect at a lifetime, that may be easier to see. Minute details, apparently inconsequential decisions and seeming coincidences coalesce over the course of time. At a distance, we can appreciate the pattern: "Ah, so that's what God had in mind!"

We may put this insight into more specific terms: "The disease was devastating, but I learned more about God and myself than I ever would have without it." "Ending the relationship with Joaquin was painful, but if I hadn't, I wouldn't have met Stevan." "At the time, changing careers seemed crazy. But knowing what I do now, I'm so glad I switched." "I don't know what possessed me to move to this part of the country—but I'm grateful that I did."

To make such comments requires the advantage of hindsight. But we can also appreciate how much we already have: the faith, gifts, skills, health, energy, family and education that have brought us to this juncture in time.

All the scripture passages about gifts of the Spirit suggest abundance; one that can be concretely visualized is the sower tossing seed with wild abandon. Although obstacles may block the seed's growth, the eventual harvest is plentiful beyond anyone's imagining. Paul VI echoes this sense of abundance: "everything we need to faithfully bring about the fullness of the reign of God is given by the Spirit through the charisms freely bestowed on all."

The *Rite of Confirmation* also states: "Christ gives varied gifts to his Church, and the Spirit distributes them among the members of Christ's body to build up the holy people of God in unity and love" (n. 22, "Homily or Instruction," p. 488).

That reassuring message restores confidence to those who doubt their own abilities, question whether they have any skills, and wonder what, if anything, they contribute to God's reign. Such insecurity is not unique to those undergoing identity crises; most honest adults will own up to such misgivings.

We may also wonder why, if God has provided for us so amply, the world is still in such a mess. Human thinkers have offered many answers to the problem of evil, some of which emerge in these lectionary readings. St. Paul suggests (Galatians 5:16-17) that humans who rely too much on themselves and too little on God misdirect their energies into jealousy, quarrels, envy and anger. Like the third servant (Matthew 25:14-20), they squander their talents. Or they hold back what they have been given, dreading the call to give all to Christ, fearing the enormous risk (Matthew 16:24).

In contrast, those who believe in their gifts acknowledge their source in God. They offer them to the community and discover outlets in an amazing variety of activities and services. 1 Corinthians 12:4-13 is a celebratory litany of spiritual gifts. The ringing affirmation could also be phrased: God hopes in you. God graces you abundantly. God is continually creating you. The Christian community needs your talents and rejoices in your gifts.

Questions for Reflection:

Why do you think we often hesitate to praise the talents God has given us?

Name one specific gift that you personally bring to the body of Christ. Do the same for your son or daughter, the candidate you are sponsoring, or the other members of your confirmation group.

What do you think is the best way to affirm another person's gift?

Activities

In the session, you reflected on the gifts you see in other people.

Which gifts of the Spirit that you see in others do you most admire?

What do you yourself most want to be? What do you long to become?

What gifts has God already given you that will help towards realizing this goal?

In what ways are you already living in the way you wish to be?

What gifts do you still wish to ask God for?

To what extent did your partner's questions help clarify your vision? Or, what did a partner point out that you hadn't known before?

Scripture

Read one or more of the following scripture passages:

- Luke 8:4-15 (Jesus tells the parable of the sower and the seed.)
- Matthew 25:14-30 (The harsh master commends the servants who made a return on their investment.)
- 1 Corinthians 12:4-13 (The gifts of the Spirit are freely given to serve the common good.)

What is your initial response to your chosen passage(s)?

Using resources from your catechist or other scripture commentary, how does your understanding of the passage(s) change?

Symbols

The Sign of the Cross

What signs of belonging have been important to you in other contexts (for example, a wedding ring, a fraternity or sorority pin, military insignia, a class ring)? What did this symbol represent?

During baptism, confirmation and each celebration of the eucharist, you are marked with the sign of the cross. What does this mean?

Read one or more of the following scripture passages.
- Luke 9:18-27 (Christians must take up their crosses daily.)
- 1 Corinthians 1:18-25 (The message of the cross looks like foolishness, but means salvation.)
- John 19:16-19 (Jesus is crucified.)
- John 20:24-29 (Thomas wants to see and feel Jesus' nail marks.)
- Philippians 2:5-11 (Jesus did not grasp at glory but humbled himself, even to the worst kind of death.)

What does the cross signify in the passage(s) you chose?

If you were to mark someone else, someone you love, with the sign of the cross, how would you explain its meaning to this person?

How does the cross bring the great hope of salvation to humanity?

Symbol

The Gift of Peace

Look in today's newspaper or watch today's newscast. Where do you find evidence of people making peace? (Examples might include international negotiation to prevent war, local efforts to curb gang violence, international efforts to protect the environment, multicultural arts festivals and concerts, negotiations between labor and management.)

Read one or more of the following scripture passages.
- John 4:20-25 (Jesus and the Samaritan woman)
- Luke 17:11-19 (Jesus cures ten lepers.)
- Mark 7:24-30 (The Syrophoenician woman calls Jesus to imagine a mission beyond the Jews.)
- Acts 2:5-21 (Different peoples hear the gospel in their own languages.)
- Acts 10:1, 30-48 (Peter sees that God shows no partiality.)

What does the passage suggest about bringing unity out of diversity?

Where do you see members of the church bringing unity or peace to today's world?

How does the church value diversity and unity at the same time? (You may wish to refer back to the newspaper or newscast mentioned before.)

Prayer

Earlier you contemplated on the vision of the person you want to be and the gifts you want from the Holy Spirit. In the light of that vision, reflect on this passage as Jesus says to you: "Ask , and it will be given to you; search, and you will find; knock, and the door will be opened for you" (Luke 11:9).

With what degree of confidence do you ask for a full outpouring of the Spirit's gifts?

What does it mean to seek with all your heart and to knock loudly?

Reflection on the Experience of the Sacrament (Mystagogy)

Reflection

The Roy children had prepared a special gift for the birthday of their recently widowed mother. A new technology enabled them to create a video of pictures from the family album. Woven together with music and captions, the photos told the story of Mrs. Roy's high school graduation, meeting her husband, their engagement and wedding, the births of their three children, the birthday parties, Christmas dinners, funerals, weddings and events that unfolded over a half-century. As the video reached its conclusion, Mrs. Roy blinked away tears and said, "We did have a good life, didn't we?"

Her experience is not unique. The couple on their honeymoon laughing at unexpected events of the wedding, the parents at a college graduation remembering the day their child was born, the widow or widower sorting belongings and recalling the memories each object prompts, the family moving from one house to another, the person celebrating a fiftieth birthday: they all engage in a common activity of looking back and reflecting before they move on.

It seems to be a distinctly human ability to discover meaning in retrospect that we might miss in the immediacy of the experience. As we clean up after a party, we delight in this person's joke or that person's surprise gift. We compare notes on which foods were most popular, and which ones we would never serve again. Long after a vacation trip, we savor the pictures and souvenirs. As one little girl commented to her mother after a weekend at the beach, "Other kids pull a dollar from their pockets; I pull out a few grains of sand."

This capacity for memory seems especially significant in regard to the sacraments. Our liturgical symbols shape our identity; the ritual actions form us into the Christian way of life. At the moment a candidate is confirmed, he might be worrying how his hair looks; she might be wondering if grandma ever found the church. Yet when we see the sacraments as beginnings, not end points, it opens up a lifetime in which to unfold their meaning.

Paradoxically, reflecting back on the sacrament thrusts us forward into discipleship. Anyone who has felt truly graced feels impelled to share the wealth in turn. For instance, a person who has spent years gathering knowledge and refining skills for a medical degree wants to use those in service to others. In the context of confirmation, we ask ourselves: Now that I have been anointed with chrism, how do I bring beauty and blessing into the lives of others? Now that this community has gifted me with peace, signed me with the cross, and laid hands upon me, how do I bring peace, saving grace and compassionate touch into my corner of the world?

While such challenging questions may be raised in our discussion groups, they will be fully answered only in our lives. Over the course of time, each candidate will discover what unique gifts he or she brings to the community. He or she will draw in different ways on the Spirit's strength and creative power. In contexts we cannot predict, in a century still unknown to us, these newly confirmed young people become the Body of Christ for the next millennium. But what greater gift can we give the future than ourselves and our young people? There we have sown our finest seeds.

Questions for Reflection:

As I reflect back over the whole confirmation preparation, what did
I do well? What might I have done differently?

What struck me most about the recent confirmation celebration?

In what sources do I find the strength and nurture to go forth and live as Christ's disciple?

Activities

Savoring the Confirmation Experience

As explained in the session, the period called *mystagogy* is for savoring the holy. We reflect back on an experience during which we might have been nervous or distracted, and appreciate it better from the perspective of time. When we are not rushed and overstimulated, we can draw out a deeper meaning through reflection.

Now that you have had more time since the celebration of confirmation and the session in which you discussed it, reflect here on the following:

What part of the celebration touched you most deeply?

In Unit 2, you described a transformation you had gone through previously. In light of the reflection on the rite during the session, look back over your life in the last few weeks or months. Name the kind of changes you see since you began confirmation preparation.

What does looking back on these changes suggest about the changes that may lie ahead in your future life as a disciple?

Scripture

Recalling the Readings

What scriptures were proclaimed during the celebration of confirmation? Your catechist or liturgist should be able to tell you the citations, or provide you with the texts. Reread them individually, and after each reading, ask the following question:

What does this text mean for me now as a disciple in action?

1st Reading:

2nd Reading:

Gospel:

Symbols

Reviewing Their Meaning

Go back in your journal to the original references for each of the following symbols. Review what you wrote there. Then answer these questions:

The Laying On Of Hands (Unit 2, p. 40)

What do you remember about this action during the celebration of the sacrament?

What are concrete ways that you can now bring the healing touch of Jesus to the people you encounter and the places you frequent?

The Anointing with Chrism (Unit 3, p. 53)

What do you remember about being anointed during your confirmation?

What are concrete ways that you can now bring the beauty and fragrance of chrism into your world?

The Sign of the Cross (Unit 4, p. 66)

What do you remember about being signed with the cross during your confirmation?

What are concrete ways you can now bring the hope of the cross into your world?

The Gift of Peace (Unit 4, p. 69)

What do you remember about exchanging the gift of peace at your confirmation?

What are concrete ways that you can now be a reconciler who brings peace to your world?

Review your journal notes in Unit 1, p. 23 under "The Eucharist," then respond to this question.

How is eucharist the time and place where your commitment to Christ is renewed and deepened again and again?

Prayer

In your own words, thank God for the people or events that have been especially helpful during your confirmation preparation. Ask God for the grace to be faithful in the future as you live out your commitment to discipleship.